Original title:
Desert Bloom

Editor: Jessica Elisabeth Luik
Author: Sabrina Sarvik
ISBN HARDBACK: 978-9916-86-495-1
ISBN PAPERBACK: 978-9916-86-496-8

Sunlit Petals

In morning light, they softly spread,
Petals of gold, the flower's thread.
Beneath the sky, a gentle sway,
Greeting the dawn, a brand new day.

Whispers of warmth, a tender kiss,
Nature's grace, eternal bliss.
In fields of green, where dreams unfold,
Stories of life in colors bold.

Through dewdrop sheen, a spark appears,
Rays of sun dissolve all fears.
In their embrace, we find our place,
A world renewed in nature's space.

Blaze of Bloom

In a field of endless light,
Flowers burst with colors bright.
Crimson, gold, and sapphire hues,
In bloom, they chase away the blues.

Flames of life, where flowers rise,
Painted in the vastest skies.
In their beauty, we find lore,
A symphony, forevermore.

Petals dance on whispers' breeze,
Soft as snowflakes, light as seas.
In their glow, the earth does sing,
A tapestry of time and spring.

Nature's Resilience

Through storms they stand, the mighty trees,
Bending 'neath the weight of breeze.
Roots dug deep in earth's embrace,
Unyielding strength and endless grace.

Mountains rise where shadows fall,
Silent guardians, standing tall.
Their peaks kiss skies of azure blue,
A testament to what is true.

Rivers carve the land with force,
Shaping paths of nature’s course.
In their flow, a song of might,
Enduring through both day and night.

Barren Beauty

In desert vast, where silence reigns,
Beauty blooms in arid plains.
Golden hues and endless sky,
Where winds of time and whispers sigh.

Sands of time, in dunes so high,
Underneath the watchful eye.
Life endures in hidden veins,
Secrets held in nature's chains.

Cacti stand in resilient pose,
Among the thorns, a flower grows.
In the stillness, life does loom,
A hidden world in barren bloom.

Heatwave Blossom

In the molten gold of summer's glow,
Petals unfurl, the heat's soft tow.
Crimson blossoms against the blaze,
Nature's answer to the sun's embrace.

Sweat drips down a sunburnt cheek,
Bees buzz in a glowing streak.
Wilted grass and scorched earth sigh,
Yet flowers bloom beneath the sky.

Mirage of color, fierce and bright,
Defying drought and endless light,
Each bloom whispers, hushed and sweet,
In the furnace, life complete.

Dusty Petals

In an arid field where shadows play,
Dusty petals greet the day.
Windswept whispers kiss the ground,
Flowers flourish all around.

Thirsty roots and sun-bleached leaves,
A stolen beauty that deceives.
Gritty air in each sighing breeze,
Through parched land, life finds ease.

Colors muted by earth’s embrace,
Desert blooms, a testament to grace.
In a world of drought and dirt,
Nature's wonders still assert.

Audacious Blossoms

Amid the cracks in concrete gray,
Audacious blossoms find their way.
Undaunted by the city’s din,
Their vibrant hues defy the sin.

Brave bouquets in urban sprawl,
Hear the silent, mighty call.
Through smog and grime they brightly thread,
Gleaming petals, endless spread.

Beneath tall towers, against all odds,
They flourish in the steel-clad pods.
Nature’s rebels, fierce and free,
In every broken place, they weave beauty.

Golden Mirage Flowers

In the desert's quiet, glowing trance,
Golden flowers start their dance.
Underneath the blazing sun,
Resilient beauty, second to none.

Sands shift and winds blow wild,
Still they bloom, forever styled.
Gilded petals catch the rays,
Turning arid days ablaze.

Mirage of gold in endless dunes,
Silent songs and whispered tunes.
Desert's heart, a floral feast,
In sparse landscapes, wonders least.

Floral Mirage

In the desert's silent sway,
Petals sprout in gold array,
Mirage blooms where shadows play,
Hues of dawn at end of day.

Cacti whisper dreams of rain,
Thorny guardians of the plain,
Rainbow blossoms break the chain,
Of the arid, endless reign.

In the mirage, colors blend,
Time and space seem to bend,
Night's cool kiss will then attend,
This floral mirage we fend.

Stubborn Beauty

Amidst the cold, the flowers rise,
Defiant blooms meet the skies,
Petals bold, no compromise,
In the frost, lie their prize.

Roots dig deep into the earth,
Clinging firm, proving worth,
Winter's chill, a painful birth,
For beauty of a stubborn girth.

Snowflakes fall, a gentle light,
Blossoms glow, pure and white,
In the cold, they hold tight,
Stubborn beauty, pristine sight.

Terra Flora

Earth's embrace soft and warm,
Cradles seeds through every storm,
Life awakes in perfect form,
Plants and flowers to transform.

Roots entwine in hidden grace,
Silent in their secret place,
Nature's dance, a tender chase,
Newborn leaves, the sun they trace.

From soil to sky, the journey starts,
Colors weave in nature's arts,
In every bloom, the spirit imparts,
Terra Flora steals our hearts.

Verdant Mirage

In the air, a verdant sheen,
Grasslands stretch, an endless scene,
Emerald waves, serene and keen,
Nature's touch in every green.

Breezes weave through leafy lanes,
Whispering secret, sweet refrains,
Echoed 'neath the sky's domains,
Verdant mirage where heart remains.

Sunbeams kiss the dewdrop's glow,
In the field where wild winds blow,
Lush and rich, the meadows grow,
Verdant dreams in endless flow.

Echoes of Moisture

In morning's hush, dew drops descend,
Whispers of night, soft mysteries blend,
On petals' edge and verdant spire,
Kisses of dawn ignite a quiet fire.

Streams of silver, secretive and cold,
Tales of twilight in their weave unfold,
Upon each leaf, a liquid dream,
Echoes of moisture in the sun's first gleam.

Scarlet Scape

In the twilight, the scarlet glows,
Among the hills where calm winds blow.
A realm where dreams and echoes meet,
Silent whispers beneath our feet.

Ruby hues in the evening mist,
Kisses from the sun persist.
Petals drift in an endless dance,
Boundless beauty in a trance.

Crimson rivers that paint the earth,
Flow with tales of ancient birth.
Soil that sings of times long past,
Vivid stories that everlast.

Mountains wear their scarlet crowns,
Majestic kings in twilight gowns.
Veils of dusk in tender drape,
Unveil the evening's scarlet scape.

Cradle of Thorns

Amidst the shadows, thistles grow,
Guarding mysteries hidden below,
A cradle of thorns, fierce and grim,
Yet life persists where light is dim.

Bruised but bold, in twilight's call,
Beauty resides within the pall,
A dance of shadows, darkly adorned,
In the cradle of thorns, new dreams are born.

Untamed Flora

Hidden realms of untamed green,
A kingdom where wild pulses keen.
Blooming secrets in sunlit rays,
Nature's art that never sways.

Vines that weave in endless spree,
Crafting paths through ancient trees.
Leaves that whisper ancient lore,
In a language soft and pure.

Petals blaze in colors bold,
Stories of the wild remold.
Fragrances that stir the senses,
Dismantling all defenses.

Roots that delve in earth's embrace,
Anchoring this untamed grace.
Songs of flora, wild and free,
A testament to life’s decree.

Sunrise Over Arid Sands

Golden star greets arid lands,
Kissing dunes with gentle hands.
Shadows fade as light ascends,
Morning's beauty never ends.

Oasis mirage shimmers bright,
A fleeting dream in morning's light.
Endless stretches of desert phase,
Bathed in dawn's embracing haze.

Cacti stand as silent guards,
Witnessing the sun's regards.
Winds that carry ancient tales,
Humming soft through sandy trails.

The desert's heart begins to beat,
With sunrise hues, the heat it greets.
An arid realm where life withstands,
The golden rise over sands.

Whispers of the Dunes

In the night, the dunes do speak,
Whispers soft and voices weak.
Secrets carried by gentle breeze,
Across the sands of endless seas.

Moonlight dances on the crest,
Of golden waves that never rest.
Echoes of the ancient lore,
Forever locked within the shore.

Footsteps fade in shifting grains,
Leaving no trace, no remains.
Ephemeral paths of those who rove,
In silent whispers, dunes' love.

Stars above and sands below,
In harmony, they ebb and flow.
Infinite tales in quiet runes,
Held in whispers of the dunes.

Ephemeral Blooms

In morning's light, a timid beam,
Petals glisten, soft and gleam.
Whispers of dawn, they gently sigh,
Beneath the canvas of the sky.

Moments fade like fleeting time,
Nature's rhythm forms the rhyme.
Ephemeral blooms in silent grace,
Leave but a trace, a whispered face.

The garden hums with hidden lore,
Beauty's dance forevermore.
Colors blend in transient rays,
Marking time in flowered days.

Fragile yet profound and true,
Ephemeral blooms in morning dew.
Life's elixir, brief and bright,
Casts its spell 'til fading night.

Untamed Beauty

Wild winds dance in fields of gold,
Stories of youth and days untold,
Beneath the azure's endless dome,
Nature's splendor finds its home.

Mountains rise, proud and free,
Secrets whispered by the talking tree,
In every crevice, life abounds,
Untamed beauty, where the heart resounds.

Cacti's Quiet Defiance

In arid lands where shadows stretch,
Cacti stand with silent fetch.
Defiant in their spiked repose,
Against the sun that fiercely glows.

No water's kiss, no fertile land,
Yet verdant hearts in silent stand.
With every thorn, a story told,
Of resilience in heat and cold.

Unyielding to the desert's whim,
In quiet strength, they never dim.
Their roots delve deep, their spirits high,
Beneath a harsh and endless sky.

A lesson in their quiet fight,
In fervent days and stark, cold nights.
Cacti rise in steadfast form,
Embracing all, enduring storms.

Blossoms in the Expanse

Across the fields, a gentle spread,
Where tulips paint the meadow red.
Blossoms whisper to the breeze,
Their soft allure puts minds at ease.

In endless rows they stretch and reach,
Beyond the eye's farthest breach.
A tapestry of nature's hand,
In every hue, serene, and grand.

Springtime’s breath invites their song,
An orchestra where all belong.
Petals dance in vibrant trance,
In this boundless, floral expanse.

Hearts ignite with nature's art,
As flowers bloom, they touch the heart.
In each field, a promise sown,
That beauty's flame is never lone.

Gritting Petals

In rocky soil, with grit unfurled,
Petals bloom, defy the world.
Against the odds, in harsh terrains,
They rise and thrive amidst the strains.

Gritting petals, colors bright,
Shine against the darkest night.
With every bloom, a tale of might,
In tough conditions, pure delight.

Nature's warriors in disguise,
In barren lands, they harmonize.
Strength and grace in union hold,
Their stories timeless, stories bold.

Each stem a testament to try,
To grasp the sun, to touch the sky.
Gritting petals turn to face,
The toughest winds with gentle grace.

Unexpected Petals

In somber skies, a miracle springs,
Unexpected petals, where sorrow clings,
Gentle hues amidst the gray,
Hope's quiet whisper, finding its way.

Through the storms, these blossoms rise,
Defying the gloom, beneath leaden skies,
A tender reminder, in nature’s prose,
That even in darkness, a flower grows.

Parchment Petals

Crisp and crinkled, delicate pale,
Burnished by the summer gale.
Whispers of a once-green tale,
Parchment petals never fail.

Etched with lines of sun-kissed time,
Nature’s parchment, pure and prime.
Fragile beauty in the grime,
Silent in their golden climb.

Dew has left them long before,
Petals laid on earthen floor.
In their stillness, offer more,
Tales of days they softly wore.

Heat-Hardy Blooms

In the blaze of midday's glow,
Stalwart flowers start to show.
Heat-hardy in their silent row,
Verses only they can know.

Sun-scorched fields, an endless wave,
Resilient spirits, petals brave.
In their steadfast, find the save,
Nature’s lesson through the grave.

Colors bold against the fire,
Thriving in the heat's empire.
Roots dig deep, yet ever higher,
Blooms endure, they never tire.

Scorching Hue

Blazing reds and oranges bright,
Caught in summer's searing light.
Petals burn in beauty's flight,
Scorching hue before the night.

In the garden, flame-tipped grace,
Passion blooms in heated space.
Each a spark, a vivid case,
Of nature's ardent, fierce embrace.

Colors dance where shadows deem,
Flowers lit by summer's beam.
In their glow, a fevered dream,
Scorching hue in sunlight's gleam.

Survivor's Blossom

Amidst the harshest drought they stand,
Flowers of a arid land.
Survivor's bloom by nature planned,
Tenacity in golden sand.

Roots dig deep, defy the dry,
Petals reaching to the sky.
In their vigor, reasons why,
Life persists though lands are sly.

In the face of summer’s wrath,
Blossoms mark a hopeful path.
Survivors in the aftermath,
Silent strength in nature’s bath.

Dusty Petal Dreams

In the garden of forgotten schemes,
Where night-blooms hush their sighs,
Dusty petal dreams arise,
In the moon's soft gleam it seems.

Time's gentle cloak envelops all,
Whispers of past linger near,
Petals fall without a tear,
In the twilight's silver shawl.

Memories drift like desert winds,
Through the canyons deep and wide,
Where the heart's regrets reside,
And the soul's journey begins.

Bound by threads of old desires,
Petals dance in silent grief,
Past and future seek relief,
In the dreaming heart's fires.

Dusty petals, whispered songs,
Linger where lost hope belongs,
In dreams where no right or wrong,
Just the heart's eternal throngs.

Skeletal Blooms

Beneath the twilight's eerie glow,
Skeletal blooms in silence creep,
Echoes of lives once so deep,
Now in ghostly gardens grow.

In the marrow of the night,
Phantom petals raise their heads,
Life and death on slender threads,
Twined within the moon’s pale light.

Whispers through the barren trees,
Ghostly gardens, silent call,
Memories of spring's bright thrall,
Haunting winds in spectral breeze.

Eyes that never saw the spring,
Gaze upon the ghostly blooms,
Silent in their nightly rooms,
Where the winds of twilight sing.

In the grave of vanished time,
Blooms arise from silent dust,
Echoes of life's fleeting trust,
In a garden most sublime.

Blooming Sands

In the desert's vast embrace,
Where the sands of time reside,
Blooming dreams in silence hide,
In the land of endless grace.

Golden dunes where secrets lay,
Whispered tales of ancient days,
In the sun's relentless blaze,
Blooms arise from the parched clay.

Hope, like flowers, finds its place,
In the heart of arid land,
Where the earth forms gentle hands,
Nurturing the bloom’s soft face.

Echoes of the past converge,
In each blossom’s brief delight,
Stories told in starlit night,
Where the blooming sands emerge.

In the desert’s silent sweep,
Petals fall like grains of gold,
Mysteries of life unfold,
In the shifting sands so deep.

Oasis Whispers

In the heart of desert's hush,
Where the weary seek reprieve,
Oasis whispers softly weave,
Through the palm’s fulsome brush.

Cool and soothing waters glide,
In the heat’s relentless chase,
Mirrored skies, a gentle grace,
In the shadow’s calm beside.

Leaves like whispered secrets sway,
In the breeze's tender hold,
Bearing stories never told,
From the night to break of day.

Mirage and magic intertwine,
In the pure and quiet air,
Whispered hopes and silent prayer,
Underneath the starry shine.

Where the weary find their rest,
Oasis whispers cradle dreams,
In the desert’s gentle seams,
Nurtured by the heart's behest.

A Mirage of Color

In the desert's heat, where sands do shimmer,
A vision bright, like sunlit glimmer.
Ribbons of hues in waves do undulate,
A mirage of color at the horizon's gate.

Golden yellows merge with reds so warm,
Purples and pinks in swirling storm.
Eyes deceive, but heart believes,
In that fleeting, vibrant weave.

As dry winds whisper secrets old,
Tales of beauty forever told.
Lost in deserts wide and grand,
A palette paints the arid land.

Where skies do meet the dunes' embrace,
Hopes arise in this painted space.
But step in close, and colors fade,
A mirage of dreams in sunlight laid.

Yet in the mind, the vision stays,
A dance of light in endless rays.
Though fleeting, it does impart,
A rainbow woven through the heart.

Succulent Symphony

Amidst the stones, where dry winds play,
A symphony of green holds sway.
Succulents in silent choir,
Resilient through the sun's strong fire.

Emerald spines and jade-like leaves,
Nature's notes in harmony weaves.
Each cactus, euphorbia's thrum,
A melody without a hum.

In arid realms where few survive,
These hearty greens do thrive and strive.
Silent songs composed with grace,
In deserts wide, they find their place.

Crimson blooms on thorny stage,
A testament to time and age.
Echoes of an ancient line,
In each succulent, textures fine.

Nature's score in muted tones,
A resilience that stands alone.
Succulent symphony, soft and hushed,
In earthen concert, blessings brushed.

Life Among Dust

Beneath the weight of endless sky,
Dust does whisper, passersby.
Life persists in quiet forms,
Amidst the dry and barren norms.

Lizards scuttle, serpents glide,
In dust and heat, they seek and hide.
A world unseen, yet teeming life,
In every grain, a silent strife.

Cacti reach with spiky hands,
Drawing life from parched dry lands.
Blooming vibrant in the night,
Stars afar, their guiding light.

Desert hares and vultures' wings,
Balance found in simple things.
Nature's dance, an ancient trust,
Survival carved in dunes and dust.

Mirage or not, the secrets keep,
Of lives that wake when others sleep.
Life among dust, resilient and refined,
Echoes of endurance, perfectly aligned.

Petals in the Wasteland

In wastelands vast, with skies so stark,
Blooms emerge, ignite the dark.
Petals whisper tales untold,
Of beauty found in deserts cold.

Roses bloom on thorny stems,
In arid winds, their grace condemns.
Vivid hues in barren sweep,
Soft secrets in the silence deep.

Poppies flare in fields of bronze,
Nestled where the quiet yawns.
Gentle blooms in harsh terrain,
Shadows cast by sun and rain.

Lilies white with purity,
Grace the landscape; harmony.
Tender blossoms bright and rare,
Resilient strength in fragile air.

In wasteland's harsh and empty room,
Petals gleam, defy the gloom.
Floral whispers, hope's command,
Life reborn in golden sand.

Abyssal Orchids

In shadowed depths, where sunlight fades,
Orchids bloom in silent glades.
Petals dark as midnight's veil,
Secrets whispered on the gale.

Roots that reach to worlds below,
Find their strength in undertow.
Silent guardians of the deep,
In their beauty, vespers keep.

Veins that pulse with hidden hues,
In this realm where darkness brews.
Spirits dance where orchids thrive,
In the night, they come alive.

Amidst the stars, they softly gleam,
Echoes of a distant dream.
Abyssal orchids, forever free,
In their grace, eternity.

Thrive Amidst Dust

In arid lands, where dry winds gust,
Life emerges, breaks the crust.
Blades of green through deserts rise,
Beneath the expanse of endless skies.

Granite landscapes, harsh and bare,
Hold a beauty, raw and rare.
Dust that shifts, a whispering sea,
Life persists with stubborn glee.

Amidst the grit, the roots entwine,
Drawing strength from ancient spine.
In the hottest, driest hour,
Blooms unfurl with secret power.

Through parched lands, a message clear,
Even here, all life holds dear.
Thrive amidst the dust and stone,
In the harsh, life finds its own.

Bursts of Beauty

From barren soil, a color springs,
Nature's magic, vibrant things.
Rays of crimson, flashes gold,
In the bloom, life's tale is told.

Unexpected, in their grace,
Bursting forth in every place.
A simple seed, a quiet start,
Creates a canvas, a beating heart.

Petals soft as summer's breeze,
Carry whispers through the trees.
Silent song of earth's delight,
In each bloom, the world ignites.

For every flower, a soul's embrace,
Delicate threads of time and space.
Bursts of beauty, fleeting, fair,
Eternal in the moment's glare.

Sun-Kissed Flora

Where dawn's first light does gently grace,
Patterns weave in warm embrace.
Petals turned to greet the sky,
Sun-kissed flora, reaching high.

Morning dews that pearls bestow,
On soft blooms, they softly glow.
Dappled light through verdant bough,
Kisses leaves as they avow.

Golden rays and shadows play,
Crafting art in light's ballet.
Each bloom so tender, kissed by flame,
In the sun, there's no the same.

Petals that in color blaze,
Reflect the dawn, the golden haze.
Sun-kissed flora, ever-bound,
In the light, their peace is found.

Floral Echoes Amongst Dunes

In whispering sands, petals arise,
Like phantoms of rain 'neath azure skies,
Soft hues of yellow, easing the brown,
A symphony blooms where windsongs resound.

Echoes of flowers past desert's hold,
Resilient hearts 'gainst sunburnt gold,
Their fleeting grace, a dance so rare,
Nature's embrace in a barren snare.

Fragrant whispers call the night,
Stars blink softly in the twilight,
Blossoms shimmer, moonlit blooms,
Silent tremors in the dunes.

Amongst the silence, fragrant streams,
Trail the dreams of old sunbeams,
Wonders grow in quiet places,
Echoing life through barren spaces.

Floral echoes paint the air,
Dunes remember, flowers dare,
To sprout in lands where none would roam,
Finding beauty, calling home.

Nature's Resilience

Amidst the storm, the roots hold tight,
Enduring winds through day and night,
With branches swayed yet never torn,
Nature's heart remains reborn.

In fields of snow, where cold persists,
Life emerges, frost resists,
Through frozen visage, blooms arise,
Proclaiming life beneath the skies.

In forests deep, where shadows play,
The cycle moves in endless sway,
Through fire, drought, and torrent's cry,
Resilience echoes, reaching high.

By rivers wild and mountains steep,
Whispers of strength in silence keep,
An unyielding pulse through years endures,
Nature's spirit, pure and sure.

In every leaf and petal small,
Adornment of resilience calls,
Life prevails through every test,
Nature's strength, in all expressed.

Scorching Blossoms

Amidst the flames of noon's embrace,
Blossoms arise with gentle grace,
Their petals bold, defy the blaze,
In deserts vast, they find their phase.

Scorching rays that sear the sand,
Cannot subdue the flowers' stand,
Resilient leaves, to sun they turn,
In this fierce heat, their hearts still burn.

Colors vivid against the grit,
A testament where life is writ,
In flaming fields, their roots hold fast,
Through trials fierce, they anchor past.

From soil dry, their buds insist,
Unyielding to the searing mist,
Amidst the dunes, they softly bloom,
Their courage brightens harshest gloom.

Blossoms thrive where few would tread,
In lands where heat and dust are spread,
A beauty forged in trials' fire,
Scorching blooms that never tire.

Thirsty Blooms

In arid climes where thirst prevails,
Blossoms seek the fleeting trails,
Of dew that graces dawn's first light,
A fragile drink for life's delight.

Through cracks in earth, their roots extend,
In search of drops where hopes ascend,
To gather sustenance from dry,
A whispered wish beneath the sky.

Their colors bright, against the parched,
Defying drought, their beauty marched,
In search of water, they persist,
With every bloom, they still resist.

Against the odds, they find their way,
In seas of dust, they dare to stay,
Their petals sing of dreams embraced,
In thirsty lands, such dreams are traced.

Thirsty blooms in deserts wide,
Declare their strength with petals pried,
From earth that holds their roots so tight,
They reach for life with all their might.

The Cacti Chronicles

In desert's stretch, the cacti stand,
With spines as fierce as shifting sand,
They whisper tales of ancient lore,
Of rains that kissed them once before.

Their shadows stretch at twilight's gleam,
Guardians of an arid dream,
Their flowers bloom in moon's embrace,
A secret in this barren place.

They weather time with silent grace,
In solitude, they find their space,
Their stories etched in thorny bark,
A testament through light and dark.

When storms arise, they bend, not break,
A silent dance for nature's sake,
They root, they rise, through endless skies,
A symbol where survival lies.

Beneath the sun's relentless glare,
In stillness, they prepare,
For moments brief when life takes hold,
And thus, their chronicles unfold.

Against the Dust

The wind it howls across the plain,
Carrying whispers, echoes of pain,
And yet with grit and steadfast trust,
They stand their ground against the dust.

The air is filled with grains so fine,
As dreams are buried, hard to find,
But hope, though frail, refuses rust,
And shines anew against the dust.

The twilight falls, a fiery shade,
Upon this vast, unending spade,
Yet night will come and dawn adjust,
Life perseveres against the dust.

In silent nights, the stars reveal,
A tapestry of wounds that heal,
As moonlight glows, so gentle, just,
They rise again against the dust.

Though time may wear and seasons grind,
In every heart, a spark defined,
The spirit soars, a will robust,
And stands unbowed against the dust.

Blooming Mirage

In the desert’s heat, where visions play,
A blooming mirage holds sway,
A garden lush, with colors fair,
Illusions crafted from the air.

Petals shimmer like morning dew,
In shades surreal, of every hue,
An oasis birthed from arid ground,
Where dreams and reality are bound.

Each flower dances in the breeze,
Though truth and trick the eye may tease,
For in this land, so dry and sparse,
A blossom hides in heart's own farce.

Yet here within this twilight gleam,
Awakes a truth within the dream,
That even in the harshest clime,
Beauty emerges, defies time.

The mirage fades with dawning light,
Yet leaves a trace of pure delight,
A memory, a fleeting page,
Of blooming splendor on life's stage.

Dunes and Blossoms

Across the dunes, where shadows lie,
Beneath a cobalt, open sky,
The blossoms wake from slumbers deep,
In sands where secrets silent keep.

They bloom despite the sun's fierce gaze,
In fleeting moments, brief displays,
A palette rich on canvas vast,
A bloom amid the barren cast.

The dunes, they shift like ancient tides,
In waves where time and wind collides,
Yet through the dance of endless grain,
The blossoms rise, defying pain.

Their petals soft in golden light,
A symbol in the desert night,
Of life that bursts from barren sea,
A whisper of eternity.

So let the sands and blooms entwine,
In harmony, a tale divine,
For in this place where harshness reigns,
The heart of beauty still remains.

Floral Scavengers

In gardens where whispers lay,
Secrets bloom in morning's hue.
Petals hunt the break of day,
Dawn brings forth a sky anew.

Thorns and roses, bond so tight,
Scavengers in quest of grace.
Bees dance softly in the light,
Harvest nectar, time to chase.

Somewhere shadows linger still,
Seeking warmth in coldest night.
Flowers claim the ancient hill,
Sunrise draws them to the light.

In the fields of endless green,
Footprints by the floral gate.
Hunters bask in unseen sheen,
Seasons weave their intricate fate.

Ghostly blooms from myths afar,
In their wake, trails remain.
Scavengers beneath a star,
Find their treasure in the rain.

Ephemeral Sands

Shifting grains beneath the toe,
Patterns lost to time's embrace.
Ephemeral sands ebb and flow,
Stars above in cosmic chase.

Waves that kiss a fleeting shore,
Moments drift like whispered chants.
Wind does write on sands once more,
Ancient tales an earthbound dance.

Ephemeral, the desert past,
Infinite, the stories told.
Sands of time can never last,
Yet to each, a dream they hold.

Footsteps fade where dunes do rise,
Marks erased by nature's hand.
Beneath the vast and open skies,
Lies the tale of ephemeral sand.

In the silence, deserts sing,
Voices from forgotten lands.
In the wind, their echoes ring,
Ephemeral, like shifting sands.

Sun-Kissed Petals

Golden rays on petals bright,
Sun-kissed gleams in morning light.
Nature's brush with hues so bold,
Crafting beauty to behold.

Vibrant dances in the dawn,
Petals soft on dewy lawn.
Silent whispers, colors blend,
Nature's canvas without end.

Every petal, sun-imbued,
Morning's kiss in every hue.
Daylight's warmth, a tender hold,
In each bloom, a story told.

Blossoms in the Dry Land

In deserts where the sun beats down,
Life finds ways to bloom and rise.
Blossoms wear a thorny crown,
Survival hides in bright disguise.

Dry land whispers ancient lore,
Stories of a thriving bloom.
Flowers' roots can reach the core,
Drawing strength from earth's own womb.

Amidst the sand, colors spread,
Vivid hues in arid space.
Tenacity in petals' thread,
Beauty lives in harsh embrace.

Beneath a sky that rarely rains,
Blossoms dance in silent cheer.
In dry land, life breaks its chains,
Thriving every passing year.

Hope will bloom where deserts lie,
Proof that life can everywhere.
In the dry land, blossoms try,
Showing beauty, rich and rare.

Echoes of Blooming Dunes

Amongst the dunes where echoes play,
Blooms arise from ancient dust.
Whispers of a warmer day,
Breaking through the twilight's crust.

Petals in the sandy seas,
Mirrors of an inner glow.
Among the dunes, the silent keys,
Unlock life's mysteries below.

Wind does carry whispered songs,
Traces of a blooming past.
In the dunes, where time belongs,
Fleeting moments, never last.

In the night, stars shed their light,
Guiding blooms through desert's tale.
Echoes whisper, soft and bright,
In the dunes, life's trails prevail.

Blooming dunes, an ageless art,
Nature's canvas, wild and wide.
From each echo, stems a heart,
Life and bloom in desert stride.

From Dust to Color

In arid lands where dust does flow,
Dreams of hues begin to grow.
Blossoms rise where none could see,
Life awakening, wild and free.

From barren ground to vibrant light,
Colors blend in dawn’s first sight.
Nature’s brush in silent sweep,
Turns the desert from dry to deep.

Every petal tells a tale,
Of where the winds and rains prevail.
From brown to green, then hues explode,
A chromatic, unseen ode.

Miracles in shifting sands,
Crafted by unseen hands.
With each bloom, in time's caress,
Nature mends, Heals and bless.

Dust now dances with the breeze,
Bearing seeds for future trees.
From earth to sky in colors bold,
The ancient story, newly told.

Sandy Petal Dreams

In deserts vast, where silence gleams,
Petals bloom in sandy dreams.
Whispers soft, a gentle breeze,
Nature's lull in golden seas.

Trailing dunes, a flower's flight,
Softly glowing in twilight.
Shadows dance on silken sands,
Mystic hues in arid lands.

Dreams of rain in petals fold,
Stories in the sands retold.
Endless skies and starlit gleams,
Craft the tales of petal dreams.

Floral Shimmers in the Heat

Golden rays upon the field,
Blooms with secrets, yet concealed.
Petals shimmer in the sun,
As the summer day is done.

Luminous with morning dew,
Mirroring the sky's vast blue.
Heat waves dance, as flowers sigh,
In the meadow's gentle cry.

Colors bold in sweltering air,
Beauty thrives with tender care.
Sunbeams kiss each velvet leaf,
Offering a sweet relief.

Shadows drift, but flowers stay,
Basking in the heat of day.
With each gleam, they softly sing,
Echoes of an endless spring.

Nature's jewels glowing bright,
Bathed in pure and radiant light.
Floral whispers, shy and sweet,
In the summer's fevered heat.

From Thorns to Petals

Among the thorns where shadows play,
Roses bloom as night meets day.
Softness hides within their reach,
Lessons only they can teach

From the harsh to gentle touch,
Nature shows us oh so much.
Thorns may guard, but petals show,
Love’s resilience in their glow.

Silent strength in every stem,
Crowning each rough diadem.
Beauty borne from piercing pain,
Grace and elegance remain.

Roses whisper through the thorns,
Of rebirth and bright new morns.
Soft surrounds the sharp and stark,
Light emerging from the dark.

Symbols of a strength profound,
Thorns and petals, all around.
In each bloom, a story’s spelled,
Through their contrast, all is meld.

Whispering Thorns

Amidst the hush of twilight's yawn,
Softly whisper tender thorns.
Secrets held in shadows gray,
Tales of dusk and breaking day.

Thorns protect the bloom's embrace,
Guarding dreams in tender lace.
Whispered echoes on the wind,
Hidden truths in shadows pinned.

Through the night, the whispers weave,
Dreams that thorns and blooms conceive.
Moonlight's touch on thorny crown,
Guides their whispers crisp and sound.

Thirsty Petals

Parched and dry beneath the sun,
Petals wait for rain to come.
Thirsty flowers aim to fall,
As they hear the storm's faint call.

Cracked earth drinks the first sweet drop,
Life will surge, and drought will stop.
Petals quiver in delight,
Drenched in nature's soft twilight.

Roots reach deep, the rain is near,
Every drop a world premier.
Thirsty stems in wet embrace,
Find salvation, beauty, grace.

From the sky, the tears descend,
Quenching souls the drought did bend.
Petals washed in liquid gold,
Stories of the storm retold.

Revived blooms in morning mist,
Each one by the raindrops kissed.
Thirsty hearts now satiated,
In the cycle recreated.

Arid Awakening

In the quiet of dawn, the desert sighs,
Beneath the cobalt sky, a secret lies.
Dusty winds carry tales from afar,
Whispers of life in each distant star.

Cactus blooms greet the rising sun,
Their vibrant hues, a battle won.
Silent strength in each thorny spire,
Nature's resolve, burning desire.

Sands shift, with patterns anew,
Ancient paths, forever true.
A lizard scuttles, seeking shade,
Stars fade as the night's parade.

Mountains stand, stoic and proud,
Guardians silent, without a crowd.
Echoes of time, etched in stone,
Mysteries deep, still unknown.

Rise and fall with the desert's breath,
Cycles of life, love, and death.
Arid yet teeming, a paradox grand,
Life's true essence, where we stand.

Petals of the Sunburnt Land

Among the dunes with whispers soft,
Sunburnt petals aloft aloft.
Glistening gold, in morning's glow,
Tales of resilience they bestow.

Flowers dance in the desert's embrace,
Their beauty found in a harsh place.
Roots run deep, in search of grace,
Sustained by nature’s timeless race.

Petals lit by the midday flame,
Each one unique, none the same.
Survival's song within each vein,
Life’s essence, passion unchained.

By dusk, a serene lullaby,
Stars fill the expanse on high.
Petals fold in twilight's hold,
Stories of warmth silently told.

Morning comes, with a bold display,
Petals greet another day.
In the arid lands, they’ll stand,
Eternal blooms, forever grand.

Floral Whispers of the Canyon

Canyon walls with shadows stark,
Floral whispers leave their mark.
In crevices, small flowers grow,
Sharing secrets from below.

Morning light casts amber hues,
Petals glisten with morning dews.
A stream's lullaby echoes near,
Bringing solace, soft and clear.

Blossoms bright in earthy fields,
Nature’s palette gently yields.
Silent sentinels in the wind,
Guardians of the places pinned.

As the day gives way to night,
Petals close, absorbing light.
A gentle hush grows profound,
In canyon’s heart, peace is found.

Whispered tales in scented air,
History’s breath everywhere.
Canyon flowers, small but grand,
Life persists in desert sand.

Tales in the Dust

Wind sings low in twilight's bend,
Dusty trails without an end.
Footprints fade, in sand they lie,
Echoes of life passing by.

In the gust, a story spins,
From where it starts, to where it ends.
Tales of travelers, long and gone,
Lives that wandered, still live on.

Hushed secrets in sunsets told,
Legends old, songs unfold.
Beneath the stars, the night reveals,
Invisible ink of tales sealed.

Cacti stand as scribes of time,
Roots deep in ancient rhyme.
In their silence, wisdom shares,
A timeless bond in quiet airs.

Morning breaks, the dust is still,
Another chapter, another will.
Tales in dust continue to flow,
In the desert's eternal glow.

Sandy Flora Symphony

Winds compose a sandy tune,
Flora sways beneath the moon.
Harmonies on desert's stage,
Nature's song on timeless page.

Cacti stand with flowers bright,
In the day and through the night.
Symphony of whispers pure,
Melodies in dunes endure.

In the hush of desert's cry,
Flora sings beneath the sky.
Every note and every breeze,
Writes a tale among the seas.

Dunes of Life

In the vast desert, sand is gold,
Whispers of time, stories told.
Footsteps vanish, lost in time,
Rhythms of life in silent rhyme.

Oases hidden, dreams unfurl,
Mirages play, shadows swirl.
The sun descends, cool embrace,
Stars ignite, a celestial face.

Winds of change, dune by dune,
Echoing the owl's soft tune.
Life persists in arid land,
With secrets buried in the sand.

Night reveals, what day conceals,
In every grain, fate appeals.
Dunes of life, rise and glide,
Endless journeys, side by side.

The Petal Rebellion

Roses bloom in defiant red,
Petals whisper words unsaid.
Against the storm, they rebel,
Silent strength, a fragrant spell.

Roots dig deep, in fertile ground,
Unseen force, they twine around.
Leaves unfurl, in sunlit spree,
Nature's song, wild and free.

Thorns protect, a heart of flame,
Beauty's price, is not for shame.
In the garden’s hush, they stand,
Testament to Earth's grand plan.

Petal rebellion, soft yet sure,
A silent fight, forever pure.
With every fall, they rise anew,
Courage found in morning dew.

Scorched Earth Florals

In the charred, relentless ground,
Where the winds of fate have wound.
Blooms arise through ash and dust,
Life reborn from layers of rust.

Scorched by trials, still they cling,
In the heart of chaos, sing.
Petals painted with earth's fire,
Born of hardship, true desire.

Flames may sear and shadows cloak,
Yet through cracks, green lives evoke.
Hope is tenacious, spirit bold,
In burned earth, tales of gold.

Resilience in full display,
Nature finds its own new way.
Scorched earth florals, bloom again,
A testament through sun and rain.

Dust Blossom Symphony

In a land of endless dust,
Where the ground begins to crust.
Blossoms burst in vibrant reams,
Nature's orchestra of dreams.

Every petal, note in air,
Harmony beyond compare.
Dust to life, they rise and play,
A symphony that won't decay.

Echoes of a time gone past,
Each crescendo, holds so fast.
In the silence, flowers speak,
Songs of strength and futures bleak.

Under sun and silver moon,
Blooms entreat in faithful tune.
Dust blossom symphony,
Frozen in eternity.

Their melody a sacred tie,
Between the earth and the sky.
In dust they find their grand display,
Through every night and dawning day.

Radiant Mirage

In desert's heart, a gleam we trace,
A phantom lake, in sunlit grace,
Where realms unseen, in shimmer, race,
A dreamscaped vision, time and space.

Mirage that dances on the sand,
A fleeting touch, an unseen hand,
In silence, whispers softly land,
Ephemeral, yet grandly planned.

Glows the sky, horizon's edge,
A sylvan art, beneath the ledge,
In silken threads, hopes we pledge,
A tranquil poem, nature's pledge.

Rays that bend, an optical show,
Bends reality, as shadows grow,
In every twist, new wonders flow,
A radiant sight, a mirrored glow.

Ephemeral as the dusk and dawn,
In fleeting moments, myths are drawn,
The desert's breath, a radiant song,
A mirage that enthralls, then is gone.

Thorns and Petals

In gardens broad, where beauty lies,
A tale unfolds beneath the skies,
Of petals soft, and thorns that rise,
An ode to contrasts, life's disguise.

Roses bright, in hues they gleam,
With fragrant notes, a tender dream,
Yet hidden sharpness, teeming scheme,
A balance struck in nature's theme.

Amidst the bloom, a vigilant guard,
To beauty's strength, we pay regard,
In thorns' tenacity, it stands hard,
Life's dual face, a paradox marred.

In every petal, soft embrace,
A secret thorn, to hold its place,
In harmony, a fleeting grace,
A dance of risk, a fateful chase.

Thus in our lives, both soft and keen,
The thorns and petals, clearly seen,
In gentle hues, and edges mean,
A garden wild, where we convene.

Dunes in Color

Amidst the dunes, a palette wide,
The colors blend and softly slide,
In desert's breath, where winds abide,
A canvas vast, horizons guide.

Golden waves, the sun ignites,
In crimson hues, the day alights,
Soft twilight blue, in fading sights,
The night descends with starry lights.

Amber whispers, gentle sweep,
In russet tones, the secrets keep,
Under moon's soft gaze, sands creep,
In vibrant dreams, the spirits leap.

Beneath the sky, in vast expanse,
A myriad shades, in silent dance,
Vermilion streaks, by sun's advance,
A chromatic tale, nature's lance.

In every grain, a story told,
In colored sweeps, the lore unfolds,
In desert's heart, vivid and bold,
A spectrum rich, in sands of gold.

Mirage Garden

In arid land, where whispers weave,
A garden blooms through eyes that perceive,
A floral dance, yet we deceive,
A spectral realm, where dreams conceive.

Echoes of green, in barren stretch,
A phantom bough, no hand could fetch,
In mind's retreat, the blossoms sketch,
A mystic grove, in thoughts, we etch.

Wilted grounds, with life imbue,
In miraged blush, the blossoms true,
Hues of hope in golden hue,
A sight surreal, yet boldly new.

The breeze that hums a haunted air,
Leaves rustle soft, in vacant stare,
A garden growing unaware,
Within our hearts, a tender care.

Yet as we step, it fades away,
A fleeting glimpse, that wouldn’t stay,
Mirage and memory, in play,
A garden lost to light of day.

Sandy Blossoms

In dunes where dreams lie still, we find,
A blossom rare in golden bind.
Whispers soft as morning dawn,
Rise where the sands have long been drawn.

Hope hides in each fragile petal’s hue,
A promise kept in arid view.
Wind does softly sing its song,
Yet roots within grow ever strong.

Each grain of sand, a timeless tale,
In desert's warm, embracing sail.
Blossoms break the barren plain,
To dance beneath the soft moon's wane.

Mirage of faith within the dry,
A gentle bloom that seeks the sky.
Amongst the endless golden sea,
The whispers of what dreams could be.

The sands give birth to nature’s will,
In barren lands, they flourish still.
A story in each petal’s spring,
A testament to life’s soft ring.

Life in the Parched Land

Underneath the sun's bright glare,
Life struggles, still, in silent dare.
Roots sink deep where none can see,
Clinging to hope tenaciously.

Cracks in earth and skies above,
Yet whispers here of lasting love.
In barren land where shadows fall,
Life's quiet resilience stands tall.

Miracles beneath our feet,
In every grain, life does repeat.
Nature's fight against the odds,
Sprouting life in desert clods.

Her resilience beneath harsh sun,
In parched lands, the battle's won.
Where life persists and dreams unite,
Against the odds, the blooms take flight.

In drought's embrace, yet life has grown,
In shadows cast, roots still unknown.
Though cracked and dry, the land does keep,
A secret strength in silence deep.

Arid Blossom Chronicle

Tales of old within the sand,
Blooming life where few have planned.
Arid winds that coarse through veins,
A testament to survival's plains.

Desert's vast and endless stretch,
Holds stories in each sunset sketch.
In the quiet of the night,
Blossoms speak with silent might.

Scorching paths and thirsty air,
Yet flowers find their roots laid bare.
In the harshest light of day,
Resilience finds its quiet way.

Stories etched in shifting dunes,
Life that hums forgotten tunes.
Miracles in colors bright,
Beneath the stars, in twilight's sight.

From the arid earth they spring,
A song of hope the blossoms sing.
In deserts wide, they flourish bold,
A chronicle in petals told.

Whispers of the Sands

Beneath the sun's relentless hold,
Stories of the sands unfold.
Silent whispers through the breeze,
Of ancient times and desert seas.

Every dune a memory spun,
Tales of battles lost and won.
Whispers carried by the wind,
Of life that sprouted, hopes pinned.

Veiled in shadows, softest tread,
Songs of life in sands widespread.
In every broken, weathered crust,
Lies tales of undying trust.

Whispers of a blooming strife,
In harshest realms of desert life.
Through the silence, whispers weave,
A tapestry where dreams believe.

In the heart of arid lands,
A secret language of the sands.
Whispers in the twilight's glow,
Of life and strength where blossoms grow.

Sand Dune Orchids

In the vast desert's golden sweep,
Silent whispers the wind keeps.
Out from the sands, gentle and grand,
Orchids bloom in this dry land.

Underneath a sun's fierce gaze,
They dance and pivot in soft arrays.
Their petals whisper tales untold,
Of resilience steadfast and bold.

When the night drapes its velvet dark,
Stars paint the sky with silver sparks.
The orchids glisten, a radiant glow,
In soft moonlight, they gently grow.

Rooted in a bed of shifting grains,
Defying droughts, outliving pains.
Against all odds, they rise anew,
Sand dune orchids, to life they grew.

In their silence, a song of grace,
Survival in this harshest place.
A testament to nature's fight,
In dunes, they bloom, pure and bright.

Emerald in the Expanse

A green gem in a sea of tan,
An oasis in the desert span.
Emerald leaves and stems so fair,
Life within this arid lair.

Fronds unfurl like a dancer's spin,
Reflecting skies, mirroring infinity within.
Midst the brightness of the day,
Cool shadows in the desert bay.

Birds descend with songs so pure,
Finding solace, their thirst to cure.
Among the stones and sunlit grace,
The emerald blooms in its rightful place.

With roots dug deep in ancient earth,
A symbol of nature's enduring worth.
Emerald in the expanse, so serene,
An enduring green, a living dream.

As the desert winds softly sigh,
Beneath the boundless, open sky.
This green gem, a beacon stands,
Emerald bright in the endless sands.

Blooming Barren

In the heart of a desert wide,
Where arid winds and spirits ride.
From the cracks of hardened ground,
Blooms of life are famously found.

Thorns and petals, a sharp embrace,
In scorching heat, they claim their space.
Beauty thrives in a harsh domain,
On barren soil, they leave a stain.

Colors vivid in the sun’s fierce glare,
A testament to life’s will to dare.
Petals soft, with stories weave,
Of ancient roots and dreams they leave.

Miracles in each tiny bloom,
In the land of sun and silken gloom.
Every flower a silent ode,
To enduring life on a rugged road.

With every sunrise, hope is spread,
In barren lands, where few have tread.
Blooming bright, they rise and fall,
Yet in their brevity, they bloom for all.

Petals in the Heat

Under skies of azure blue,
In a world where nothing new.
Petals rise in desert heat,
Nature's pulse in rhythmic beat.

Crimson shades and colors bright,
Against the sun's relentless light.
Petals whisper, soft and sweet,
Life persists in every beat.

Scorching days and cooling nights,
Doomed to endless, fierce fights.
Yet they open, one by one,
Petals reach towards the sun.

Mirrored in the scorching sand,
A promise of a softer land.
In each bloom, a silent voice,
Declaring life's enduring choice.

Petals in the heat stand tall,
Their beauty answers nature's call.
Against the odds, profound and neat,
Life persists, in desert's heat.

Bloom in the Void

In the darkness, seeds find embrace,
Seeking light in boundless space.
Whispers of time, quietly trace
The journey of a flower's grace.

Roots entangle soil so deep,
Silent promises they keep.
Through the shadows, they will creep,
Awakening life from dormant sleep.

Petals unfurl in night's dark chime,
Creating beauty, a rhythm in rhyme.
In the void, they bide their time,
Blooming anew with each new climb.

The void, a canvas vast and free,
A miracle of eternity.
In every bloom, a silent plea,
For light, for love, for you, for me.

Petals of the Basin

In the basin's gentle curve,
Water's dance begins to swerve.
Petals float, no more reserve,
Nature's heart starts to observe.

Lilies dreaming in the dusk,
Fragrance carried by the musk.
Golden hues, nor rich nor brusque,
Speak in whispers soft yet brusk.

Basin mirrors clear and deep,
Secrets that the waters keep.
Petals dance, as if in sleep,
A story told in silent weep.

Every drop, a world within,
Echoes where the petals spin.
In the basin, life begins,
In ripples, in waves, we find our kin.

Floral Wilderness

In the wild, flowers roam,
Finding ways to call it home.
Petals shine in nature's tome,
A tapestry in gilded foam.

Amidst the thorn and ragged leaves,
Beauty tangles, interweaves.
Secret paths it gently cleaves,
In the wild, the heart believes.

Blossoms brush against the sky,
Whispers nature's lullaby.
Colors burst as moments fly,
Through the wild, the flowers cry.

Each one tells a different tale,
Of the winds and whispered gale.
In the wild where dreams set sail,
Floral secrets we unveil.

Sizzle and Blossom

Summer sun with tender heat,
Warms the ground beneath our feet.
Plants arise where rays do meet,
In the sizzle, life is sweet.

Blossoms born from golden rays,
Dance in light through endless days.
Colors vibrant, bright displays,
Nature's art in sunlight's blaze.

Heat and bloom, a fervent kiss,
Moments wrapped in fragrant bliss.
The sun and flowers, naught amiss,
In their sizzle, there's no abyss.

Blossoms whisper to the sun,
Songs of growth, their anthem spun.
In their dance, they're never done,
Blooming bright, till day is won.

Floral Mirage

In the desert's endless sprawl,
Where shadows gently fall,
A mirage of blooms appear,
Whispers in the arid air.

Petals kissed by phantom dew,
Colors painting skies so blue,
Oasis blooms in dreams unfold,
Stories ancient, yet untold.

Fragrance wafts on summer breeze,
Silent prayer among the trees,
Mirage holds its fleeting grace,
Ephemeral, like a lover's face.

The winds they dance, the sands they sing,
Of ephemeral blooms and fleeting spring,
In desert's heart, a vision lies,
Vanishing beneath the skies.

Transient beauty, a siren's call,
In the desert vast and all,
Floral mirage, fantasy's kin,
A moment's glimpse, a dream within.

Sands of Awakening

As dawn breaks o'er the shifting sands,
Light spreads over arid lands,
The desert wakes from slumber deep,
Secrets hidden in its keep.

Whispers carried on the breeze,
Among the stones, the ancient trees,
Dusty paths reveal their lore,
Echoes from the days of yore.

Sunlight paints the dunes aglow,
Patterns in the grains below,
Life unseen begins to stir,
In nature's arms, they softly purr.

Awakening to morning's kiss,
Desert blossoms in silent bliss,
Mysteries held in golden grains,
Eternal in the sunlit plains.

Rise and shine, the desert's creed,
A timeless tale its souls can read,
In sands of waking, life anew,
Every dawn a curio blue.

Cacti Serenade

In twilight's soft and gentle fold,
A tale of strength and warmth is told,
Cacti stand with arms outspread,
Guardians of this earthen bed.

Their needles sing a song of rain,
Echoes through the arid plain,
Whispers dance with desert's breath,
Connecting life, defying death.

Beneath the stars, their secrets weave,
Stories that the winds conceive,
Roots dig deep in ancient grounds,
Silent songs their heart surrounds.

Moonlight drapes them silver bright,
Jewels sparkling through the night,
Nature's fortress, green and true,
Cacti serenade the blue.

Resilient spires in desert's clasp,
In the silence, they still gasp,
Serenade of life so pure,
Cacti’s strength forever sure.

Blossoms in the Barren

In the barren, harsh and stark,
Where no comfort leaves a mark,
Blooms emerge, defy the strain,
Life erupts from stress and pain.

Tiny petals, frail yet bold,
Stories of the desert told,
Color in the desolation,
Hope within the isolation.

Summer's breath is fierce and wild,
Still they flower, nature's child,
Miracles in dusty beds,
Resilient, lifting weary heads.

Amidst the rocks and thorny press,
Life springs forth to convalesce,
Blossoms in the barren stead,
Power from where fear had fled.

In the desert, blooms decree,
From struggle comes vitality,
Barren lands with life adorned,
In courage, nature is reborn.

The Sands Awaken

Beneath the dusk, where shadows lie,
The grains of time begin to fly.
Each whisper of the desert breeze,
Untangles secrets from the seas.

Footprints fade beneath the stars,
The moonlight mends the day's old scars.
Whispers weave through ancient lore,
The sands awaken, forevermore.

Golden dunes that shift and twirl,
Carrying dreams from distant world.
With every breath, a tale is spun,
Embracing both the moon and sun.

Mirages dance, the eye deceives,
But truth in twilight heart believes.
In this realm of sand and sky,
Eternity and moments tie.

In the hush of morning light,
New dreams take wing, and shadows fight.
Endless tales the sands will tell,
In silence, where the spirits dwell.

Floral Phantoms

In garden dark, where moonlight spills,
A world of phantoms starts to thrill.
Petals shimmer, spectral grace,
Whispers haunt this twilight space.

Ghostly blooms in silver light,
Blossoms pale, a ghostly sight.
Each flower a tale of yore,
Echoes from the days before.

Midnight breezes through the leaves,
Stirring softly, magic weaves.
Phantoms rise in floral form,
In this realm, unseen, they swarm.

Glowing softly, ethereal gleam,
As if from a forgotten dream.
Dewdrops gleam, like spirits' tears,
Wonders lost to countless years.

As dawn's first light begins to break,
Phantoms fade, the day to wake.
Yet in darkness, they remain,
Floral phantoms, dreams unchained.

Floral Beacons of the Sands

In deserts wide, where shadows play,
Amid the dunes, the flowers sway.
Beacons bright in arid land,
Their colors like a painter's hand.

Petals bloom where life seems none,
Beneath the harsh and blazing sun.
Each blossom tells a tale of hope,
In a world where life must cope.

Cacti guard their floral crown,
Glistening in the golden gown.
Their brilliance calls the weary soul,
Guiding hearts towards a greater goal.

Amidst the sand, a vibrant hue,
Life persists where skies are blue.
Hope in petals, bright and grand,
Floral beacons of the sands.

In the harshest realms they bloom,
Breaking free from nature's tomb.
Against the odds, they stand and shine,
Testaments to life divine.

Silent Dune Petals

On dunes where silence reigns supreme,
Petals whisper like a dream.
Each one a solitary voice,
In the quiet, they rejoice.

Desert's breath, a gentle sigh,
Carries whispers to the sky.
Petals tell of things unseen,
Stories stitched with golden seam.

Moonlight casts a silver veil,
Over dunes so vast and pale.
Petals glow with mystic light,
Softly in the still of night.

Silent blooms in twilight's hue,
Echoes of a world subdued.
In their silence, truths unfold,
Tales of wisdom, soft yet bold.

Morning breaks, the petals close,
Hidden where the stillness grows.
Yet in silence, they remain,
Guardians of the desert's reign.

Grit and Grace

In quiet shadows, strength does gleam,
A spirit fierce, a silent dream.
Through storms and trials, unshaken, bold,
In every heart, a story told.

With steps though weary, still they pace,
The endless dance of grit and grace.
The world's vast weight, no burden made,
In every touch, a moment staid.

From burning plains to frigid heights,
The soul endures, ignites the night.
In tender whispers, power found,
In gentle ways, unyielding ground.

The hardest stones, by streams embrace,
Erode to beauty, time and space.
So too, the heart, with whispered care,
Becomes a jewel, beyond compare.

When gently falls the final veil,
A tale of grit and grace prevail.
The echoes linger, soft and free,
A legacy through eternity.

Oasis Blossoms

In desert's heart, where shadows fall,
An oasis blooms, a gentle call.
Amid the sands, life finds a way,
In purest drop, thc dawn of day.

Mirrors of sky in quiet pools,
The weary travelers, soothing cools.
A refuge found in endless strife,
An unexpected burst of life.

Whispering palms guard precious peace,
Their grace and shade, the soul's release.
Wildflowers paint the golden dunes,
Their fragrance dances with monsoons.

Here dreams revive, hopes reappear,
An emerald glow, so crystal clear.
The soul drinks deep, in joyous breaths,
Amidst the quiet, life bequeaths.

As twilight blends with dawn’s embrace,
The oasis whispers of its grace.
To all who seek and wander lost,
A gentle gift, a gentle cost.

Thorns of the Mirage

In endless sands, illusions bloom,
A phantom touch, a whispered gloom.
Oft promises of sweet relief,
Entice the heart, betray belief.

With every step, the vision shakes,
A shift of hope, a cruelest break.
The stark horizon, false and bare,
A thorned promise, hung in air.

Mirages cast their wicked spell,
Like sirens' song, their whispers dwell.
To lead astray the weary soul,
A fleeting glimpse, a tarnished goal.

Yet in that dance of light and shade,
A truth within the false conveyed.
The heart grows wise with every turn,
In mirage's vanishing, we learn.

Though thorns may prick and scratch the dreams,
They pave the path where vision leans.
In every fall, the soul's ascent,
The thorns of mirage, gift of lament.

Sunset Flora

As day descends, the colors blend,
In twilight's kiss, a gentle mend.
The flowers bow to evening's grace,
In sunset's glow, a soft embrace.

Petals whisper of day's farewell,
In fragrant sighs, their secrets tell.
The garden hums a lullaby,
Beneath the painted, tender sky.

Shadows stretch as stars ignite,
An onyx canvas, flecked with light.
The flora seeks the moon's soft glow,
In night's embrace, they softly grow.

Each bloom reflects a twilight's hue,
A fresco bathed in evening dew.
As darkness wraps the world in peace,
Their silent breathings never cease.

In twilight's realm, the flora dance,
A symphony of night's romance.
So end the days in peaceful streams,
In sunset's flora, fade to dreams.

Milton Keynes UK
Ingram Content Group UK Ltd.
UKHW022239280824
447491UK00010B/284

9 789916 864968